Thirty-Three Ways to Help with Writing

Thirty-three Ways to Help with Writing equips teachers and teaching assistants with a wide range of practical resources to help children who are having difficulties learning the basic skills of writing.

Offering a range of activities and games to engage children and encourage motivation in the classroom, this essential companion provides ready-to-use material that doesn't need lengthy forward preparation.

These practical and fun ideas incorporate a variety of learning styles, using kinaesthetic and auditory techniques, which put the emphasis on 'games' rather than 'work'. The activities are especially suitable for teaching assistants working with individuals or small groups. *Thirty-three Ways to Help with Writing* works step-by-step through practical activities which:

- keep children motivated and enjoying learning
- do not require extensive knowledge or experience from the adult
- are adult-led so children don't have the opportunity to repeat mistakes
- are grouped into different basic skills so teachers can choose the activity best suited for the child's needs
- have clear, concise and pedagogically sound reasons for the activity
- include an extension activity where appropriate, to challenge pupils.

The Routledge *Thirty-three Ways* series of practical 'how-to' books is for primary teachers, teaching assistants and SENCOs who are in need of fresh ideas to teach pupils who are struggling with basic skills. Although aimed mainly at primary age pupils, secondary teachers will also find this book invaluable to use with pupils who are falling behind. The series facilitates good inclusive provision and is a resource from which useful ideas and materials can be taken without having to plough through chapters of theory and research.

Raewyn Hickey is an experienced classroom teacher who has worked in both the Literacy Initiative for Teachers project in Westminster and as a consultant for the Primary Strategy.

Thirty-Three Ways to Help with . . .

Supporting children who struggle with basic skills

Series Editor: Linda Evans

This series of practical 'how-to' books is for teachers, teaching assistants and SENCOs who are in need of fresh ideas to teach pupils in their care who are struggling with basic skills. It provides them with the tools to make good provision for a range of children in their class, and is planned to be a resource from which they can extract ideas and materials without having to plough through chapters of theory and research.

All titles are A4 in format, photocopiable, and include an introduction, and a double-page-per-activity layout. A template at the end of the book will help teachers keep a record of which activities have been used with each child and how well they achieved, and this will feed into the IEP/statement process.

Written by experienced practitioners and experts in their respective field, this series will be a life-line to anyone who at times finds teaching children who are struggling a bit of a struggle.

Other titles in the series:

Thirty-Three Ways to Help with Numeracy by Brian Sharp
Thirty-Three Ways to Help with Reading by Raewyn Hickey
Thirty-Three Ways to Help with Writing by Raewyn Hickey
Thirty-Three Ways to Help with Spelling by Heather Morris and Sue Smith (forthcoming)

Thirty-Three Ways to Help with Writing

Supporting children who struggle with basic skills

Raewyn Hickey

Routledge
Taylor & Francis Group

LONDON AND NEW YORK

First published 2010
by Routledge
2 Park Square, Milton Park, Abingdon, Oxon OX14 4RN

Simultaneously published in the USA and Canada
by Routledge
270 Madison Avenue, New York, NY 10016

Routledge is an imprint of the Taylor & Francis Group, an informa business

© 2010 Raewyn Hickey

Typeset in Bembo and Franklin Gothic by
Keystroke, Tettenhall, Wolverhampton

Printed and bound in Great Britain by
MPG Books Group, UK

British Library Cataloguing in Publication Data
A catalogue record for this book is available from the British Library

Library of Congress Cataloging-in-Publication Data
Hickey, Raewyn.
 Thirty three ways to help with writing : supporting children who struggle with basic skills / Raewyn Hickey.
   p. cm. — (Thirty three ways to help with)
 1. English language—Composition and exercises—Student teaching (Elementary)
 2. Language arts—Remedial teaching. I. Title. II. Title: 33 three ways to help with writing. III. Title: supporting children who struggle with basic skills.
 LB1576.H3449 2010
 372.62′3—dc22   2009034069

ISBN10: 0–415–55340–7 (pbk)
ISBN10: 0–203–85838–7 (ebk)

ISBN13: 978–0–415–55340–7 (pbk)
ISBN13: 978–0–203–85838–7 (ebk)

Contents

C. Improving contents: Fiction writing Activities:

D. Exploring different forms of writing: Non-fiction Activities:

Thirty-three ways to help . . . the series

This is a series of books to help teachers, teaching assistants and parents who want to help children to learn.

Most children, at some stage or other in their school life, come across something that they find difficult; a small minority of learners have difficulty in grasping the basic ideas presented in many lessons. Whichever the case, there is a need then for extra explanation and practice so that children can unravel any misconceptions, understand what is being taught and move on. Very often nowadays, this extra practice – or 'reinforcement' – is provided by teaching assistants (TAs) who are such a valuable resource in our schools.

Planning activities for TAs to use with children who need extra help can be challenging, however. There is little time to design 'mini-lessons' for TAs to use with individuals or small groups of children – and to talk them through the 'delivery' of such activities. This is exactly where the **Thirty-three ways to help** . . . series comes into play.

Teachers will be able to choose an appropriate activity for individuals or groups as part of their structured programme, or as a 'one-off' lesson for extra practice. The games and activities require no prior theoretical reading or knowledge and little or no preparation, and can be easily used by TAs or volunteer helpers in the classroom; teachers may also wish to share some activities with parents who want to know how to support their children at home. The activities use a multi-sensory approach to learning – visual, auditory and kinaesthetic; they have been designed for children aged 6–11 years, who need additional help with particular skills and concepts.

Teachers are constantly challenged to find ways to keep pupils moti-vated and to give them worthwhile 'catch-up' opportunities. But much of the photocopiable material available to teachers is too often 'busy work' which keeps children 'occupied' as opposed to learning. The books in this series provide a variety of adult-led activities that will keep children interested and take them forward in their learning. In this way, their confidence and self-esteem will grow as they experience success and have fun at the same time.

Series features

- Activities are practical (do not involve pencil-and-paper worksheets) and multi-sensory, to keep children motivated and enjoying learning.

- Activities do not require a lot of preparation and any materials required are provided or readily available in classrooms.

- Activities are adult-led so children do not have the opportunity to keep repeating the same mistakes.

- Activities are grouped into different basic skill areas, so teachers can choose the activity best suited for the child's needs.

- Clear, concise reasons are set out for each activity.

- Extension activity is given where appropriate, to challenge pupils and extend their learning.

Acknowledgements

I would like to thank Mrs Avril Topping, Associate Adviser at Warrington, the staff of Ravenbank Community Primary School at Lymm, and Kara for allowing me to trial the activities included in this book and for giving me such valuable feedback.

Introduction

It seems that every school is concerned with raising the results in writing. Learning to write is a complex, developmental process, but, like any craft, it can be taught and learnt, even if some children need more help and encouragement than others.

However, looking at text structure or 'powerful' verbs in isolated exercises does not necessarily lead to children improving their writing. An emphasis on this type of activity may help children gain a superficial understanding of a grammatical feature, but it will not lead to an improvement in children's writing overall, unless the exercise is followed by a writing experience where the children are expected to include it in their composition.

Children's writing will improve when they can read from a 'writer's point of view'. Using an analytical approach on the premise 'you need to see it and hear it before you can use it', the best way to improve children's writing is through a three-stage teaching sequence:

1. Shared Reading – exploring the language and structure of a text.

2. Shared Writing – shared composition, supported writing or teacher demonstration.

3. Independent writing – putting what has been taught into practise.

If any of these steps are missing, then your teaching of writing will not achieve the best results.

This book is designed to help those children who, for whatever reason, have been unable to make the connection between what they have seen and how they can best use what they have seen and make it their own.

- This book is divided into sections relating to the skill being taught. Each section begins with an introduction explaining why the skill has been included and giving an indication of where the skill fits in terms of National Curriculum levels for writing.

- The order of the activities is not intended to indicate a sequence of teaching.

- The tasks and games require children to be actively involved in their learning and to use logical, rhythmic, visual and kinaesthetic intelligences to make the learning memorable and fun.

- Adult supervision and/or involvement is essential in consolidating a child's learning.

Commercially published reading or writing programmes/schemes provide a glossary of terms nowadays – make sure that all teaching staff, assistants and helpers are familiar with these: parents, too, will appreciate having this information. (There is also a glossary provided at the back of this book.)

Note: Throughout this book a child is referred to as 'he'. This is not to suggest gender bias but is used merely as a way of improving fluency in the text.

A. Beginnings

The following activities are included to help those children who are struggling to compose a sentence. At a National Curriculum Level, these activities are best suited for those children working towards and working within Level 1.

Phonics

As the teaching of phonics is taught through a sequential programme, no attempt is made in this book to replicate games and activities designed for the specific teaching of hearing sounds in words.

Letters, words and sentences

We use the terms *letter*, *word* and *sentence* frequently when teaching children, assuming they understand the difference. For a small number of children, these words are interchangeable; they haven't understood that letters make up words and words make up sentences.

The activities *Sorting Game* and *From Letters to Sentences* have been included to help these children.

Teaching words

With the current emphasis on teaching letter sounds, you can expect children to be able to sound out words as they write, especially the frequently used two- and three-letter words which are phonetically regular (am, it, but, can). However, children need to remember several things when sounding out words – the sound relating to each letter, where it comes in the word and how to form the letter, all of which takes a lot of concentration. For some, learning a few essential, frequently used words 'by heart' is important in order to free up a little of their brain power to be able to pay attention to other important writing skills such as the structure of the sentence, remembering what they want to write, and writing it in a logical sequence.

Knowing how to write some words instantly is important because a beginner writer needs to:

- Feel successful as a writer. A child feels the greatest sense of satisfaction as a writer when someone else can interpret his writing.

- Use less energy than is required by sounding out every word he writes.

The adult should:

- Choose which words to teach using:

    a. The words the child has almost got right, e.g. wnet (went) teh (the).

    b. The child's guided reading book. As the child adds a new, frequently used word to his reading vocabulary, he should learn to write it at the same time.

    c. There are a number of lists of high-frequency words. The words taught may be chosen in any order but should always match with what the child is reading.

- Teach only one word at a time.

Children who find it hard to remember need to build up a bank of words slowly to begin with, or they will forget the words they learned the day before or last week.

Make sure the children can write and read all the previously learned words before teaching a new one.

- Teach a new word that uses different letters to the previously taught word.

Children would become easily confused if *my* was taught next after *me*.

Sorting game

This is a way to practise the terms 'letter', 'word', 'sentence' and understand what they mean.

Resources

- Copies of pages 5 and 6.

Preparation

- Photocopy pages 5 and 6, cut out and either paste each piece on to individual cards or laminate.

- Space the heading words across the table face up. Keep three of each of the letter, word and sentence cards and scatter the rest face down on the table.

Activity

- Point to each of the heading words and read them to the child.

- Place a letter, word and sentence card face up in front of the child.

- Name each one, e.g. *This is a letter, this is a word.*

- Help the child sort the three cards. **The child does not need to name the letters or read the sentence or words.**

- Let him practise again by putting the two sets of the three cards in front of him.

- Ask him to sort the cards on the table under the headings letter, word, sentence.

Extension

- Write several sentences on a piece of paper or photocopy a piece of text.

- Give the child three different coloured highlighters.

- Ask him to mark a letter with one colour, a word with another and a sentence with the other.

Sorting Game

Heading cards

Letter	Word	Sentence
A m k	*go*	*I go to school*

Letter cards

s	*h*	*m*
t	*y*	*w*
d	*v*	*e*
a	*g*	*r*

Sorting Game

Word cards

is	*he*	*my*
to	*the*	*we*
dad	*on*	*for*
and	*go*	*went*

Sentence cards

Here is my teddy.	*I can see a bear.*	*This is my book.*
I went to the shop.	*I played on the swing.*	*We are at home.*
Dad drives a van.	*I can climb the tower.*	*I got an ice-cream.*
Look at me in the car.	*I am going on a plane.*	*I went to Nana's.*

From letters to sentences

This is a way to learn the terms 'letter', 'word', 'sentence' and what they mean.

Resources

- Magnetic or plastic letters.
- Paper and pencil or small whiteboard and pen.

Preparation

- Put the following letters on the table: a m g o t e y h.

Activity

- Say, *These are called letters.*
- Demonstrate how you can make words from letters by putting two letters and then three letters together to make *am go me to my he the,* explaining how the same letters are used over and over again to make different words.
- Use the magnetic letters to make the following words with the child's help:
  - can (letters to make a friend's name, e.g. Tom, Emma, Ben) see we.

- Demonstrate how to use the words in a sentence, explaining about leaving gaps to show where one word ends and the next begins.

- Place some letters and words on the table and ask the child to name which are letters and which are words.

- Say, *We are going to write a sentence, putting letters together to make words and then putting the words together to make a sentence.*

- Help the child decide on a sentence.

- Ask the child to rehearse the sentence he is going to write two or three times and count the number of words.

- Draw a line for each word on the page, leaving gaps for the spaces, e.g. The child's sentence is: *My cat is black and white.* The paper would have six lines:

_____   _____   _____   _____   _____   _____

- Ask the child to write each word using the sounds he knows. Write in the letters he is unable to hear.

- Use the magnetic letters where the child isn't sure of how to write the shape, or can hear the sound but doesn't know the letter.

- Use both letter names and letter sounds throughout this activity. 'A (letter name) makes a (letter sound) sound', e.g. an 'ess' makes a 'sssss' sound.

Extension

- Ask the child to compose a sentence.

- Rehearse it and count the number of words.

- Ask the child to write down the sentence without drawing the lines for each word. Encourage him to know when the word is completed so that he can leave a space before beginning the next word.

Instant writing

This is a way to help children write the most frequently used words.

Some children have difficulty remembering which word is which when they come to write it. This activity helps the child by providing prompts.

Resources

- A whiteboard and pen.

Preparation

- A list of three or four words the child has been learning.

Activity

- Ask the child to write the first word on the whiteboard. If the child hesitates, or writes a different word, write it for them.

- Ask, *What do you notice about the letters in this word?*

- Encourage the child to notice something about the beginning or end of the word he is having difficulty recalling, e.g.

  - *the* has two tall letters

  - *go* has a letter with a tail at the beginning

- *my* has a letter with a tail at the end

- *went* has four letters; it starts like 'we'

- *like* has a tall letter, a short letter, a tall letter and a short letter.

- Ask the child to write down the word he is having difficulty remembering at least four times, encouraging him to write it quicker each time.

- Keep using the prompts until the child can write the list of words without hesitating.

Children can become discouraged if:

- They are left too long trying to remember.

- The adult says '*Come on, you remember, we did it yesterday.*'

Extension

- Allow the child just a fraction longer before giving the prompt.

- Begin the prompt and don't quite finish it, e.g. *It has a tall letter, then a short letter, then a . . .*

Disappearing words

This is a way to practise writing the most frequently used words.

Resources

- A list of the words a child can write independently.

- Water.

- A clean paintbrush.

- Paint – three to four colours and a brush for each colour.

- A large (A3) piece of paper.

- Access to a paved outside area.

Preparation

- Choose four to five words the child has learnt to spell recently.

Before beginning the activity

- Tell the child he is going to paint the words he can write by himself.

Activity

- Say, *We are going to take the water and the clean paintbrush outside to write some words that will disappear.*

- In an outside space, say, *I am going to give you a word and I want you to write it on the concrete.*

- Ask the child to write the words you have chosen using the paintbrush and water.

- Ask for each word more than once.

- Ask the child to move to different places to write. Ask him to read the words before they evaporate.

- (Back inside) say, *I am going to say a word and I want you to write it on the paper with paint. You choose the colour you want to use.*

- Ask the child to write the words he wrote outside using paint. Ask for each word more than once.

Extension

- Ask the child to write the words he knows in a list down the page.

- Use a timer and ask the child to write the words before the timer runs out.

Musical stops

This is a way to learn where to put capital letters and full stops.

Resources

- Three or four library books or the child's reading books.

- A bell, triangle or other musical instrument for the child.

Preparation

- Copy four sentences from one of the books on to paper or a whiteboard.

Activity

- Say, *I am going to read you some sentences. I want you to listen and when I have finished, I want you to tell me if I stopped at all while I was reading.*

- Read the passage to the child at your normal reading pace.

- Ask him if he heard you stop at all. If not, repeat the reading, exaggerating slightly the pauses between the sentences.

- Give the musical instrument to the child.

- Say, *I'm going to read the sentences again. This time, when you hear me stop, I want you to play your instrument once.*

- Read the passage, giving the child time to play a sound.

- Ask, *How many times did you play your instrument? Did you play a sound at the end?*

- Repeat the reading as many times as it takes for the child to hear where each sentence ends.

- Show the child the paper or whiteboard. Ask, *I've got the words I am reading on this paper. Can you see anything on here that is the sign that tells me when to stop?*

- Help the child find and name the full stops. Ask, *What can you tell me about the next word (after the full stop)?*

- Help the child identify and name the capital letter after the full stop. Say, *Are there full stops and capital letters in every book we read?*

- Give the child the books and ask him to check some pages for full stops and capital letters.

Extension

- Ask the child to think of a movement he could make to show a full stop, instead of playing an instrument. What movement could he make to show a full stop is followed by a capital letter?

- Choose another four sentences to read. As you read, ask the child to indicate where the full stops and capital letters come in the passage by making the movements he has chosen.

Full stop game

This is a way to help children notice full stops and capital letters.

Resources

- A copy of the Full stop game board on page 17.

- One dice.

- One counter for each player.

Preparation

- Photocopy the blank Full stop game board on page 18 and paste on to card or laminate.

Rules

- A player throws the dice and moves his counter the corresponding number of squares.

- If his counter lands on a square with a capital letter, he moves forward one space.

- If his counter lands on a square with a full stop, he misses one turn.

- The winner is the first person to reach the Finish square.

Activity

- Say, *Today we are going to play the Full stop game.*

- *First, put your counter in the start square.*

- Ask the child to throw the dice and move the corresponding number of squares.

- Then take your turn.

- If either the child's or your counter lands on a square with a capital letter or a full stop, explain the rules: Capital letter – move forward one square. Full stop – miss one turn.

- Continue the game until one person reaches the Finish square.

Extension

- Photocopy the blank Full stop game board on page 18.

- Write letters, words or sentences in the spaces using capital letters and full stops.

Full Stop Game

Start	E	b	f	•	G	L	d	G
								h
O	m	C	•	h	u	p	A	T
•								
D	e	N	•	s	t	m	k	u
								w
Finish	•	r	R	n	B	•	l	y

Blank Full Stop Game

Start								

Finish								

B. Writing longer, more interesting sentences

Fiction writing

These activities are most suitable for those children working towards, or who have just attained, National Curriculum level 3. One way of improving writing is by adding or changing words in a sentence.

Teaching grammar

The teaching of grammar has become part of the writing programme, not in order for children to be able to parse sentences, but for children and teachers to have a common language in which to be able to talk about texts.

Children need to have a basic knowledge of word classes because:

- When teaching style, the nouns change according to the formality of the text, e.g. *Edward Harper* is more formal than *dad* or *Ted*.

- When taking notes, nouns are important to retain the essential meaning of the text.

- Adjectives are used extensively in some types of writing such as advertisements and persuasive writing.

- Although adjectives can give more information, children need to learn how to use them selectively. Overuse makes the writing laborious to read and the adjectives themselves lose their impact.

- Children need to learn how to avoid weak or overused verbs.

- Consistent use of verb tenses helps cohesion in writing.

- Verbs often effectively describe the mood or feelings of a character.

- Verbs are important in writing figurative language. *The wind sighed and moaned through the trees.*

- Adverbs are used to intensify the verb in advertisements and persuasive texts.

- Adverbs can be moved around in a sentence to greater or lesser effect.

- Connectives help to give cohesion to writing by extending sentences and linking paragraphs.

Activities

The following activities are included to help children understand how the language they choose has an impact on the reader.

- Writing longer sentences by:

    a. using connectives

    b. adding description using adjectives and adverbs.

- Choosing specific words in order to:

    a. make the writers' meaning clear

    b. depict an image of characters, settings and moods

    c. develop children's individual styles

    d. write in both informal and formal styles.

Verbs in action

This is a way to learn how to choose interesting verbs for impact.

This activity uses verbs of one word. Verbs made up of more than one word are introduced in Snakes and verbs on page 27.

Resources

- Blank paper or whiteboard and pen.
- Card or paper cut to make approximately 12 word cards.

Preparation

- Ask the child to think of a person, e.g. baby, child, dad, mum, grandparent, and write on whiteboard.

Before the activity

- Say, *The activity we are going to do is about using interesting verbs.*
- Write the following sentence on the board: *The boy tripped over the step.*
- Ask the child if he can identify the verb in that sentence. The verb is the word that names the action.
- Repeat using: *He splashed through the puddles.*

- Write other sentences if the child is still unsure.

- Explain that the verbs are in the past tense – the action has already happened. Ask the child to look at the verb, e.g. *tripped, splashed*. Explain that the verb is in the past tense. Ask how the ending of the verb is changed to make the verb into an action that is happening.

- He . . . *(tripped* becomes *trips; splashed* becomes *splashes).*

Activity

- Return to the whiteboard and remind the child of the person they chose at the beginning.

- Ask the child to think of things that person could be doing.

- Write the verbs on the word cards, one word for each card, and arrange to form a list.

- Then ask the child to name places where the person might be.

- Write the places on cards, one clause for each card, and arrange in a list to the right of the verbs.

- Ask the child to rearrange the cards to match the action to the place, e.g. *climbs up a hill, splashes in the swimming pool, sulks at the playground.*

- Read the clauses with the child.

- Say, *Maybe there are other verbs we could use so the verbs and places begin with the same letter. If we can't change the verb, perhaps we can change the place,* e.g. *climbs up a cliff, sulks at the swings.*

- Extend the child's vocabulary as much as possible.

Extension

- Return to the clauses written previously. Add any more that the child may think of.

- Rearrange the ideas into a catchy three-line rhythm and add a fourth line to make a verse.

   Pesters to go to the playground
   Sulks by the swing
   Slips down the tall slide
   Trying everything.

Walk this way

This is a way to help children choose verbs that make the most impact.

A game for three or more players.

Resources

- Whiteboard or large piece of paper and pen.

- A copy of Walk this way cards on page 26.

Preparation

- Photocopy page 26 and cut into cards. Place the cards in a pile on the table.

Before beginning the activity

- Say, *Before we can begin to play Walk this way, we need to write down some verbs that we use to show how people walk. We can walk slowly. Stand up and walk slowly.*

- Ask the children to think of a verb that means to walk slowly.

- Write the words in a list under the heading *walking slowly.*

- Repeat the same process with verbs to *walk quickly, softly* and *angrily*. You may need to use a thesaurus to introduce the children to a wider vocabulary.

- The children may think of the following:

walk slowly	walk quickly	walk softly	walk angrily
plod	scamper	tip-toe	stomp
shuffle	hurry	creep	stamp
trudge	dart	sneak	clump
slog	dash	sidle	march
traipse	scurry	patter	

Activity

- Ask the first child to take the top card off the pile and then look at the words in the list under the same heading. Ask him to choose a word and keep it in his head.

- Ask the child to then walk around in the manner of the word he has chosen.

- Ask the other children: *How is (name) walking? Look at the words in the list we have made under the heading (of how he is walking). Which word do you think best describes how (name) is walking?*

- Once the children have found the verb the player is thinking of, cross it off the list.

- Repeat, giving each child a turn, or until all the cards have been used.

Extension

- Ask the children for verbs that mean *said*.

- Make sure you get a range that covers the different moods people may be in when they speak: *quickly, softly, angrily, loudly*.

- Write each word on a card (see table below for ideas).

- Write a list of verbs as before.

- Decide on a sentence for the children to say as they perform the action.

The children may think of the following:

speak quickly	speak quietly	speak angrily	speak loudly
gabble	whisper	bark	bellow
babble	murmur	growl	shout
jabber	sigh	snarl	yell
prattle		grumble	scream
			roar

Walk This Way Cards

walk slowly	walk quickly	walk softly
walk angrily	walk slowly	walk quickly
walk softly	walk angrily	walk slowly
walk quickly	walk softly	walk angrily

Snakes and verbs

This is a way to learn that verbs can occur in chains.

Resources

- A copy of Snakes and verbs board on page 30.

- A copy of Snakes and verbs sentences on page 31.

- Whiteboard and pen.

- One dice.

- One counter for each player.

Preparation

- Photocopy the Snakes and verbs board and laminate or paste on to cardboard.

- Photocopy the Snakes and verbs sentences and cut into cards.

- Place the cards face down in a pile.

- Write the following sentences on the whiteboard: *The teacher looked at the children. It was a wet playtime. They were sitting reading comics at their desks.*

Rules

- A player throws the dice and moves his counter the corresponding number of squares.

- If his counter lands on a square with a snake's head in it, he picks up a sentence card. If the sentence on the card contains a verb chain, he is safe. If, however, the sentence has just one verb, the player must slide down the snake.

- The winner is the first person to reach the Finish square.

Before beginning the activity

- Tell the child that today's game is about verbs. Say, *The verbs used in the* Verbs in action *and the* Walk this way *activity were action verbs. The verbs are 'doing' something. However, some sentences contain verbs that don't 'do' anything at all. All sentences have a verb, but some sentences have two or even three verbs one after the other. We call them a* **verb chain.**

- Ask the child to look at the sentences on the whiteboard and identify a sentence which has an action verb; a sentence with a verb that doesn't 'do' anything; and a sentence with a verb chain.

Activity

- Say, *Today we are going to play a board game called* Snakes and verbs.

  First, put your counter in the start square.

- Ask the child to throw the dice and move the corresponding number of squares.

- Then take your turn.

- If either the child's or your counter lands on a square with a snake's tail, say, *When you land on a snake's head you have to pick up a card. Read the sentence. Find the verb or verbs. Does the sentence have a verb chain? If it does, leave your counter where it is. If it does not, you must slide down the snake.*

- Continue the game until one person reaches the Finish square.

Extension

- Play the game as before but add cards with the following sentences. The player may stay on the snake's head if the sentence uses a verb chain or verbs like *is, was, have.*

  - I had a cold.

  - No one was at the door.

  - My name is Anna.

  - Ben has a sore foot.

  - We have ice-creams at the beach.

Snakes and Verbs

Finish	30	29	28	27	26
	21	22	23	24	25
	20	19	18	17	16
	11	12	13	14	15
	10	9	8	7	6
Start	1	2	3	4	5

Snakes and Verbs Sentences

I listened to the music.	They were playing football.
A raindrop fell on my head.	It could be cold in the night.
I heard thunder.	Lightning is flickering across the sky.

The lizard curled his tongue.	Polly had been frightened.
Henry gazed out the window.	Polly was scared.
Will shut his eyes.	Someone could have seen him.

A noun crossword

This is a way to show how choosing the best noun gives a reader a clearer image.

Resources

- A copy of the noun crossword on page 34.
- A pencil.
- A thesaurus.

Preparation

- Photocopy the crossword.

Activity

- Talk about what a crossword is, and that there is one letter in each square.

- Show the child the thesaurus and talk about how it is useful for finding words that mean almost the same thing – *synonyms*.

- Look at the title of the first crossword – *wind words*.

- Talk about which word to look up in the thesaurus (wind) and help the child fill in the crossword, showing him how the letters from one clue help with another one.

Extension

- Find *noise* in the thesaurus.

- Read the words with the child and talk about which word would best describe the quietest of the loud noises; the loudest noise; list them in order of loudness.

- Look up *rain*.

- Think of times when you have been caught in the rain. Which word would best describe it?

Crossword Answers	
Wind words	
Across	**Down**
1 hurricane	2 breeze
3 gale	
Water words	
Across	**Down**
1 stream	2 river
3 brook	4 pond
Thief words	
Across	**Down**
1 burglar	2 rustler
3 pickpocket	

Noun Cossword

Wind Words

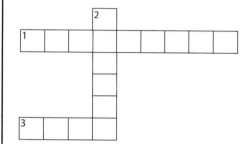

Clues

1 across	A very strong wind that can blow over trees and houses
3 across	A wind that howls around the house and makes the windows shake
2 down	A gentle wind that just moves the leaves on the trees

Water Words

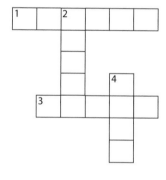

Clues

1 across	Water flowing between banks you could almost jump over
3 across	A trickle of water between banks you could jump over
2 down	Water that is usually wide and often deep
4 down	Water in a shape that is usually small and round

Thief Words

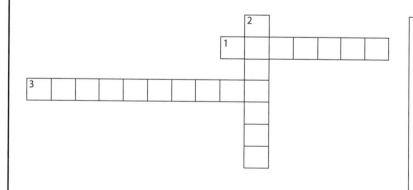

Clues

1 across	A thief who sneaks into places to steal things
3 across	A thief who steals things from bags and pockets
2 down	A thief who steals animals from farms

Rob the nest

This is a way to learn to recognise nouns and verbs.

A game for three or four players, or multiples of three or four players.

Resources

- A copy of Rob the nest words on page 38.
- Four hoops for three players five hoops for four players.
- Access to an outdoor area or large space.

Preparation

- Photocopy the words. Cut up and laminate or paste on to cards.
- For three players, spread three hoops in a triangle with a fourth hoop in the centre.
- For four players, spread four hoops in a large circle with a fifth hoop in the centre.
- Scatter the cards face up in the centre of the circle.

Rules

The game with three or four players

- Each player stands behind a hoop.

- The adult calls either *nouns* or *verbs*.

- The children run into the middle of the circle and take *one* card with a noun (or verb) written on it.

- If all the noun cards are gone, players can steal a card from another player's hoop.

- The game continues until the adult calls *stop*.

The game with six, eight or more players

- The children form a team behind each hoop. They number themselves 1 and 2 or 1 to 4.

- The adult calls either nouns or verbs, and also calls a number, e.g. Nouns. Number 2.

- That player runs to the centre hoop to take one card.

- At any point the adult can change the number called out, giving other team members a turn.

- The players can steal from other hoops.

Activity

- Explain the rules to the children. Remind the children not to stand in the hoops – they are likely to get a foot caught when they run.

- If there are two or more players in each team number them 1, 2 and so on.

- Have a trial run to make sure the children have understood the rules.

- Repeat the game as often as you like.

- Award points for the team which has collected the most correct cards at the end of each game.

Extension

- Play the game using verbs and adjectives or verbs and verb chains.

Rob the Nest Cards

table	climb	sausage
summer	jumped	is seen
river	bring	temper
happiness	make	crept
Hall Road	was late	air
clouds	shouting	slides
circle	whistled	passed

An adjective poem

This is a way to practise using adjectives for description.

Resources

- A2 size paper or large whiteboard and pen.

- Pictures of frogs (optional).

Preparation

- Copy the following on to A2 size sheet of paper or whiteboard.

  _____ _____ _____ frogs

  _____ _____ _____ frogs

  _____ frogs too.

  _____ frogs _____ frogs

  _____ _____ _____ frogs

  Don't forget _____ frogs

  But if I could choose,

  The best of them all,

  I'd have _____ frogs.

Activity

- Begin by asking the child to think of a frog.

- Say, *Think of some adjectives to describe what a frog looks like (colour, legs, feet, eyes).*

- You may need pictures of different types of frogs for inspiration.

- Ask the child for adjectives that describe how a frog feels to touch.

- Make a list of the adjectives down one side of the paper.

- Look at the poem together and choose adjectives for each line.

- The poem may of course be adapted for any creature (or other noun).

Extension

- Look at the poem again.

- Look for different ways of grouping the adjectives.

- Do any of the adjectives begin with the same letter? E.g., *small, slimy, smooth.*

- Is it possible to have adjectives on each line that begin with the same letter (alliteration)?

  e.g.   small, slimy, smooth frogs

  bulging eyed, black spotted, big frogs.

Adjective antonyms

This is a way to practise using adjectives for description.

Resources

- A copy of the Adjective antonyms story on page 43.

- A thesaurus (optional).

- A highlighter pen.

- A pencil.

Preparation

- Photocopy the Adjective antonyms story.

Activity

- Read the passage to the child.

- Ask the child to read it with you a second time and mark all the adjectives with the highlighter.

- Working through from the beginning, change each adjective to its opposite (antonym) and write it above the original word.

- Read the text again and enjoy how the meaning has changed.

- Some thesauruses have antonyms listed at the end of each word entry; you may want to make use of this.

Extension

- Choose a passage from the child's reading book, class book or library book and find the adjectives. Write the antonyms on a separate piece of paper. Read through again, substituting the new words for the adjectives in the text, and see how the meaning changes.

Adjective Antonyms Story

Once there was a clever dolphin who liked to splash about in the waves as they curled up the beach.

One day, he was happily playing when, all of a sudden, an enormous wave loomed up behind him. The little dolphin tried to dive under the huge wave as it came crashing down, but it picked him up by his short tail and hurled him right up on to the beach. The small dolphin lay stunned, gasping on the shore. The hot sand burnt his skin. The noisy seagulls flew up to laugh at him.

"Silly dolphin," they sneered. "Don't you know you are too small to play in the big waves? Now look at you. You're stuck."

"Help. Please help," cried the dolphin. "I'll die if I stay on this horrible sand."

One or two of the seagulls tried to help, but their wings were too soft to push.

The dolphin felt sick and miserable.

Suddenly he heard a friendly voice.

"My good friends and I can help you," it said.

The unhappy dolphin felt something pinch his short tail. He looked behind him and saw dozens of fat crabs crawling up the sand. Some burrowed underneath him, others grabbed his tail. The squawking seagulls flapped and fussed, getting in the way as the crabs strained and heaved. The crabs pulled and they pushed and they carried the little dolphin until he was back floating in the warm sea.

"A big cheer for the dolphin," cried the seagulls, who had short memories.

"A big cheer for the crabs," yelled the dolphin as he flicked his tail and disappeared under a little wave.

© R Hickey 2010 *Thirty-three Ways to Help with Writing* Routledge

Signing off

This is a way to practise using adverbs for description.

Resources

- A2 size paper or large whiteboard and pen.

- A thesaurus.

Preparation

- Ask the child to think of characters in traditional tales, e.g. Goldilocks, the wolf, Jack, the ugly sisters.

Activity

- Begin by asking the child to think of the ways people finish off formal/business letters,

  e.g. Yours faithfully Yours sincerely.

  Ask, *If Goldilocks had to write a letter to The Three Bears to say sorry for breaking into their house, how do you think she would feel as she wrote it?*

  Possible answers could be: *ashamed of herself, sorry, reluctant, guilty, humiliated.*

- If the child finds it difficult to think of words, look up one of the ones given, for example, *ashamed*, in the thesaurus.

- Write the words on the paper.

- Tell the child that these words are adjectives. Choose one of the adjectives from the list made previously. Ask the child to read the following, and change the adjectives into an adverb. Repeat with another adjective from the list.

Goldilocks wrote the letter (*sad*) sadly

(*sorry*) sorrowfully

(*reluctant*) reluctantly

feeling very ashamed (adverbial phrase).

- Write the adverbs on the paper or board. Say, *So instead of ending her letter, Your friend, or Yours sincerely, Goldilocks might write Yours reluctantly, because she didn't really want to write the letter. Or Yours sorrowfully because she really is sorry.*

- On the paper write: Goldilocks: *Yours* _____ (ask the child to choose the one they liked the best.)

Choose another character and repeat the exercise.

Extension

- Choose one the characters from the activity above.

- With the child's help write a letter as if you were the character to someone else in the story/solicitor/town council/social welfare.

- Use one of the adverbs to end the letter.

Moving adverbs

This is a way to show how adverbs can give different emphases, depending on their place in the sentence.

Resources

- A copy of the poem on page 48.

Preparation

- Photocopy the poem.

- Photocopy the poem in the table and cut along the lines. Keep each line of the poem in a separate pile.

Activity

- Tell the child that this is an activity using adverbs.

- Read the poem together.

- Give the child the first line of the poem cut into three, and ask him to reassemble it.

- Ask, *Can you find one part of that sentence that you could move to another place?*

- Give the child the opportunity to discover that an adverb can move to different parts of the sentence.

- Repeat with the second, third and fourth lines.

- Tell the child that the word he is moving is an adverb.

- Ask the child to move the noun and the verb cards to different places. Does the sentence still make sense?

- Ask, *What becomes the most important part of the sentence when the adverb is at the beginning? What becomes more important when the adverb is at the end?*

  Slowly the snail creeps over the ground – the speed is important.

  The snail slowly creeps over the ground – the snail is more important than the speed.

  The snail creeps over the ground slowly – the snail on the ground is more important than how fast it is going.

Extension

- Choose a book that has a paragraph which includes adverbs. Read the passage with the child. Identify the adverbs. Try moving the adverbs to different places in the sentence. Can all adverbs move?

- Ask the child to think of things that move slowly (or quickly). Write them down in the style of *Hunting*. It is not important for the lines to rhyme.

Moving Adverbs Poem

Hunting

Slowly the snail creeps over the ground,

Quickly the thrush peers all around,

Slowly the cat sneaks, belly to dirt,

Quickly the thrush swoops,

Who'll get there first?

Poem to cut up

slowly	the snail	creeps over the ground
quickly	the thrush	peers all around
slowly	the cat	sneaks
quickly	the thrush	swoops

Connectives card game

This is a way to learn how to expand sentences using simple connectives.

Resources

- A copy of the sentences on page 52.

- Copies of the connectives on page 52.

- A copy of the sentence beginnings and endings on pages 53 and 54.

Preparation

- Photocopy the sentences on to white paper and cut up into cards.

- Photocopy the sentence beginnings on to red paper and the sentence endings on to blue paper.

- Cut up into cards.

- Place the sentence endings in one pile, the sentence beginnings in another and the connectives in a third pile.

Before beginning the activity

- Place the cards face up in front of the child. Say, *Today we are going to play a game called the Connectives card game. First, we are going to join some sentences using* but *or* because.

- Read the sentences with the child.

- Ask him to choose two sentences that could go together. Say, *We want to join those two sentences together to make one sentence. Would you join them using 'but' or 'because'?*

- Ask the child to read the sentences using the connective he has chosen.

- Repeat the activity until you are sure the child has understood which connective to use for the sentences to make sense.

Rules

- Divide the cards containing the sentence beginnings between the players.

- Place the cards with the sentence endings and the connectives in front of the players in two piles.

- In turn, each player chooses the top card from the sentence-ending pile, and the top card from the connectives pile.

- If the player can make a sensible sentence by adding the connective and the sentence ending to one of his sentence beginnings, he can have another turn.

- The winner is the child who is able to make the most sentences.

Activity

- Say, *Now we are going to play the Connectives card game. First, spread your sentence-beginning cards in front of you.*

- Ask a player to take the top card from each of the two piles.

- Ask him to read through the sentence beginnings in front of him, and to add the connective and sentence ending.

- Ask, *Does the sentence make sense?*

- If a sentence makes sense, the player joins the three parts together and is allowed another turn, e.g.

| I like wet play | because | we can play board games. |

Extension

- Prepare six cards with *if* written on them and six with *and also*.

- Use the sentence starters below and ask the children to choose the connective *if* or *and also* and then to complete the sentence appropriately.

  - We are going to the zoo . . .

  - Pet rabbits need food . . .

  - It's my birthday soon . . .

  - I can climb trees . . .

  - The chair might break . . .

  - He finished his work . . .

Connectives Card Game Sentences

I want to go for a swim	*it is very hot*
I like cooking	*I hate having to tidy up*
We have to stay inside	*it is raining*
I want to go out and play	*I like jumping in puddles*

Connectives

but	*but*	*but*	*but*
but	*but*	*but*	*but*
but	*but*	*but*	*but*
because	*because*	*because*	*because*
because	*because*	*because*	*because*
because	*because*	*because*	*because*

Sentence Beginnings

I like wet play at school	*I went to the dentist*
Yesterday we went on a train	*I play football on Wednesdays*
I like swimming in the sea	*I like holidays in the summer*
I fell down the steps	*I am nine years old*
I hate going shopping	*I love swimming*
Mum was cross	*Dad was late for tea*
The tree branch was broken	*I went to the pictures*
We don't have a dog	*I got a present*

Sentence Endings

we can play board games.	I broke my tooth.
we went to see Grandma.	my sister goes to dance lessons.
Mum likes swimming in a pool.	Gran likes holidays in autumn.
they were wet and slippery.	my sister is only five.
my sister loves it.	I don't like water up my nose.
I spilt paint on the carpet.	the car had a flat tyre.
it was very windy.	my sister stayed home.
we have two cats.	it was my birthday.

Connectives to and from

This is a way to learn how to use connectives to join two sentences.

Resources

- A copy of Connectives to and from game board on page 58.

- A copy of Connectives to and from sentences on page 57.

- One dice.

- One counter for each player.

Preparation

- Photocopy the Connectives to and from game board and laminate or paste on to card.

- Photocopy to and from sentences and cut up into cards.

- Place the cards face down in a pile.

Rules

- A player throws the dice and moves his counter the corresponding number of squares.

- If his counter lands on a square with a connective written in it, he picks up a sentence card. If the sentences on the card can be joined using the connective, he is safe. If, however, the sentences cannot be joined using that connective, the player moves back two spaces.

- The winner is the first person to reach the Finish square.

Activity

- Say, *Today we are going to play a board game called Connectives to and from.*

  First, place your counter on the start line.

- Ask the child to throw the dice and move the corresponding number of squares.

- Then take your turn.

- If either the child's or your counter lands on a square with a connective,

Say, *When you land on a connective you have to pick up a card. Read the two sentences. Can you make the two sentences into one sentence by inserting the connective? Does the sentence make sense? If it does make sense, leave your counter where it is. If it doesn't make sense, move your counter back two spaces.*

- Continue the game until one person reaches the Finish square.

Extension

- Read some of the child's recent writing together. Ask the child to find sentences that could be made into one sentence by using a connective.

- Play the Connectives To and From game again but this time:

  - If a player's counter lands on a square with a connective written in it, he picks up a sentence card. If the sentences on the card can be joined using the connective at the beginning, the player stays on the square. *The player can read the second sentence before the first.* If the connective cannot be used at the beginning of the sentence, the player moves back two spaces.

- The winner is the first person to reach the Finish square.

Connectives To and From Sentences

We have to go to bed. We have tidied away our toys.	We go to bed. We have a bath.
Mrs Jones opens the shop. It is nine o'clock.	I get out of bed. Mum calls me for breakfast.
Dad drives to work in the car. It is raining.	Sam does not go to school yet. He is nearly five.
Sam won't get out of bed. She is late for school.	I feed my rabbit. I have my tea.
I have to go to bed. I am not tired.	We can't go swimming. Mum can go with us.
Peter was naughty. He was sent to bed.	We are going to a party. We have been to school.

Connectives To and From Game Board

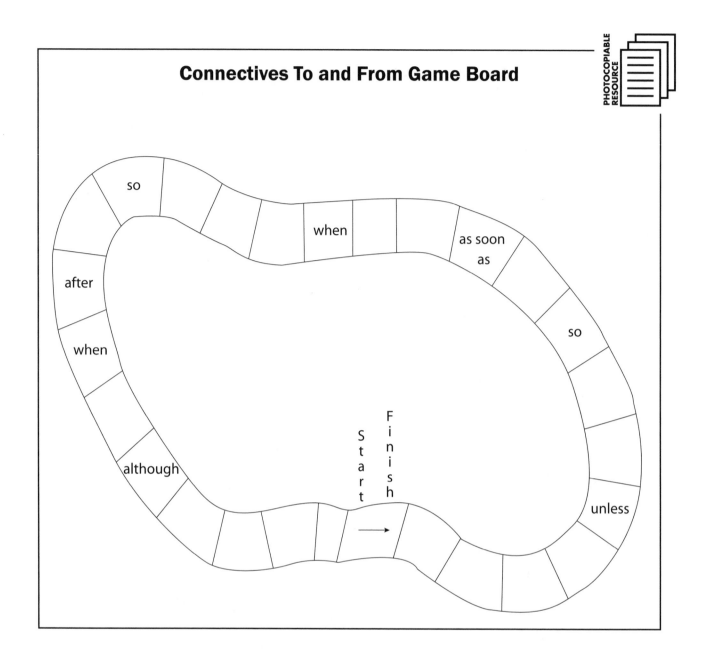

Fiction writing

Keeping the reader interested

These activities are best suited for those children who have attained National Curriculum level 3 and are working towards level 4.

Sophisticated writers use a range of techniques to keep their readers engaged.

1. Beginning sentences and paragraphs in different ways.

2. Adding clauses and phrases for more information.

3. Using varying lengths of sentence.

4. Implication. E.g. The snow was thick and solid, piled against the wheels of the parked cars and walls. Colin pulled his woollen hat down over his ears (implying: It was cold).

5. Concealment. E.g. I heard *something* on the stairs.

6. Characterisation through speech, e.g.

'Sorry I'm late,' Erica began. 'First of all we all slept in. The alarm didn't go off or something. And then there was no milk for breakfast and I had to run to the shops and then . . .'

'Enough,' sighed Mr Burt. 'You're here now. Please sit down.'

7. Original similes and metaphors.

Activities

The following activities are included to help children think like writers and understand some of the techniques writers use to keep the reader interested.

Musical sentences

This is a way to help children use phrases and clauses to add more information.

This is a game for four or more children.

Resources

- One chair for each child and two extra chairs arranged in a circle/ square facing inward.

- A copy of Musical sentences on pages 63–65.

- A musical instrument such as a triangle or drum.

Preparation

- Photocopy sentences and cut up into cards.

- Put the cards from group 1 face down on each chair.

Activity

- Explain to the children that they are going to play a game like musical chairs except that in this game there are more chairs than there are children.

- Ask the children to walk around inside the chairs to the beat of the musical instrument. When it stops, ask them to pick up the card from the nearest chair and sit down.

- Ask them to read their cards and join other children to make a group of cards which can make a sentence.

- Ask the children who have not been able to join a group, if they are able to move any part of the sentence to another place.

- Give points to the children who composed the sentence and moved the positions of the cards.

- Play the game again, asking the children to make sure they don't stop at the same chair.

- Repeat the game with cards from groups 2 and 3.

Extension

- Read two or three of the sentences from the game above.

- Help the children to compose a sentence together by asking them to think of:

  a. a person/animal

  b. what he/it is doing

  c. how he/it is doing it

  d. where this thing is being done.

- Repeat the exercise but this time ask the children to compose their own sentences.

Musical Sentences

Group 1

over in the meadow	a frog	lay her eggs
in the pond	out at sea	made a nest
to an old oak tree	a squirrel	scrambled
a nut in his mouth	rapidly	on the sand

Group 2

its brakes squealing	*a train*	*pulled*
into the station	*between its jaws*	*along the road*
to the ship	*the tugboat*	*was attached*
by a steel cable	*as it guided the ship into dock*	*as it ran onto past the post*

Musical Sentences

Group 3

her bottom lip trembling	Deeta	*threw her bag*
tears in his eyes	Mahmud	*too heavy*
stood up	Mum	*to the bullies*
running out of patience	*yelled at her son*	*by lunch time*

Connect 3

This is a way to give children more information by adding clauses and phrases.

Resources

- Photocopy of page 68.

Preparation

- Cut up the photocopied sheet into noun, verb and phrase cards.

- Mark the backs of the noun cards A, the verb cards B and the phrase cards C.

- Deal out cards A and B evenly between the players.

- Place cards C face down in a pile.

- Players sort their cards face up into two lines, nouns and verbs.

Rules

- The first player takes the top card from the pile.

- If the player can make a sensible sentence using any card from A and B with the card from the pile, he can keep it.

- If the card cannot be used, the player discards it.

- The winner is the first person who can use all of his cards in a sentence.

Activity

- Say, *Today we are going to play a card game called Connect 3.*

- Deal cards A and B to players and begin the game, asking the first player to take the top card from the pile and to either keep or discard it.

- When the game has finished, choose a sentence from each player and ask the children if the C card can be moved to another place in the sentence.

Extension

- You will need small whiteboards and pens for each person.

- Write short sentences, using a noun and a verb, on a whiteboard to show the child.

  E.g.

  a. The boy ran.

  b. The dog barked.

- Ask the child to write down a phrase to go with the sentences.

- Ask him if he can write down more than one phrase for each sentence.

Connect 3

A

A crow	The cat	The man
A woman	A goat	The boy
The girl	The baby	The dog

B

sprinted	stretched	fell asleep
ate	called	tripped
yawned	cried	scratched

C

first of all	at the same time	after a while
down the road	at the post office	in the garden
through the town	in the forest	away from the house

All change

This is a way to help children write longer sentences using different techniques.

Resources

- A copy of All change game board on page 72.

- A copy of All change sentences and cards on page 71.

- One dice.

- One counter for each child.

Preparation

- Photocopy the All change game board and either paste on to card or laminate.

- Photocopy the sentences and instructions. Cut up into cards and either paste on to card or laminate.

- Choose *one* sentence card for the game and place it at the bottom of the game board.

- Place the instruction cards face down in a pile.

Rules

- A player throws the dice and makes the appropriate number of moves. If the counter lands on a hexagon that contains a star, the player picks up a card from the pile. He reads the sentence at the bottom of the board, then changes the sentence according to the directions on the card.

- If the player is able to change the sentence according to the instructions, he moves on three spaces. If the player cannot change the sentence he stays where he is until his next turn. He does not throw the dice, but chooses another instruction card.

Activity

- Explain to the child that he is going to play a board game. Show him the board, point out the stars and explain what he has to do if his counter lands on a star.

- Show him one or two of the instruction cards.

- Practise following the instructions before beginning.

- Play the game following the rules above.

Extension

- Choose one of the child's reading books.

- Lay three or four instruction cards from the All change game face up on the table.

- Read one of the instruction cards and ask the child to scan the text to find a sentence that uses the grammar in the instruction.

- Ask the child to write a sentence following one of the instructions.

All Change

Sentences

The boy hurried	A policeman drove the car	The squirrel ran

Instruction cards

Begin the sentence with an adverb	Add a connective and a phrase	Begin the sentence with a connective and add a clause
Add 'while' and a phrase or clause	Begin sentence with Although . . . and add a phrase/clause	Add an adjective
Add a phrase to tell 'how'	Add a phrase to tell 'where'	Begin the sentence with As soon as . . . and add a phrase or clause
Add an adjective	Add an adverb	Add an adjective

All Change

Start

2

1

4

6

3

5

11

9

7

12

10

8

14

16

18

13

15

17

23

21

19

24

22

20

26

28

30

25

27

29

Finish

Non-stop sentences

This is a way to help children with characterisation by using speech.

A game for four or more players.

Resources

- Access to outdoor area or large space.

- Freestanding large whiteboard.

- A pen.

- Cones to mark out a track.

- Marker to show where player is to stand.

Preparation

- Divide the children into two teams: a writing team and a running team.

- Mark out a circular running track with cones or similar markers.

- Place a marker away from the running track to indicate where the first writer is to stand.

- Place the whiteboard and pen by the writer's marker.

Illustration

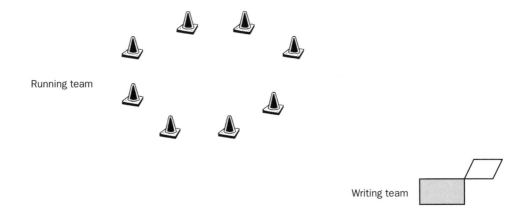

Running team

Writing team

Rules

- The running team lines up behind the first marker of the circular running track.

- The writing team lines up behind the writer's marker.

- On the call of '*WRITE*' the first runner races around the circuit and back to where he started.

- At the same time the writer begins writing a sentence on the whiteboard.

- The writer must stop as soon as the runner returns to base.

- As soon as the first runner returns the second runner runs the circuit while the second writer continues the uncompleted sentence.

- The aim is to make the sentence as long as possible. The writing team is 'out' when a player completes the sentence or the sentence becomes nonsensical.

- The teams change sides – the writers become runners and the runners become writers.

- The winning team is the one with the most words in the sentence.

Activity

- Tell the children they are going to play a game that is similar to Non-stop cricket, only with writing involved instead of a bat and wickets.

- Explain the rules of the game and divide the children into two teams.

- Keep a note of how many words each team writes in their sentence before they are 'out'.

Extension

- Choose one of the child's reading books. Choose a page and ask the child to scan it for the longest sentence.

- Ask the child to think of a sentence similar to the one in the book. Set a time limit and ask him to compose the sentence before the time runs out.

NB. When working with just one or two children, use some sort of timer or clockwork toy instead of 'runners'.

Cinderella simile

This is a way to help children use similes in their writing for additional description.

Resources

- A copy of page 78.

- Large whiteboard or piece of paper and a pen.

Preparation

- Photocopy page 78 for each child.

- Write the following on the whiteboard:

  - as white as snow

  - as hard as a rock

  - eats like a bird

  - fought like cat and dog.

Activity

- Explain that these are similes – where an object is compared to something else. Similes use 'as' or 'like'. Talk about any common similes the child may know.

- Ask the child to think about the sun and how it is often described.

- Write the following on the whiteboard:

  - *The sun was like a . . .*

  - *It was as hot as . . .*

  - *The sun beat down like . . .*

- Ask the child to think of words to complete a simile for each line.

- Ask the child if he remembers the story of Cinderella. Ask him to retell it quickly.

- Give a copy of page 78 to the child and help him to write similes in the spaces.

Extension

- Choose a different traditional tale which the child knows.

- Write a part of the story together, putting in as many similes as possible, such as the Cinderella simile.

Adjective Antonyms Story

Cinderella sat like a _____ in front of the fire. Her two stepsisters who were as ugly as _____ had gone to a ball at the palace. Cinderella wished she could have gone too.

Suddenly there was a noise like _____ and an old fairy appeared. She was as round as _____ and had a nose like a _____.

"I am your Fairy Godmother," she said.

Cinderella laughed like _____ when her Fairy Godmother turned a pumpkin into a coach and four mice into footmen.

Cinderella left for the ball. As soon as her stepsisters saw an unknown beautiful girl step into the ballroom they went as green as _____ with envy.

The prince immediately asked Cinderella to dance.

"You dance so beautifully," the prince told her. Cinderella gave him a smile like _____.

© R Hickey 2010 *Thirty-three Ways to Help with Writing* Routledge

Six sizzling sausages

This is a way to help children think about alliteration.

This is a game for two or more players.

Resources

- Access to an outside area or large space.
- A hoop for each player.
- A dice for each player.
- Card and pen.

Preparation

- Cut the card into eight pieces and write the following words, one word on each card:

  tiger, puppy, wind, cat, sand, monster, tornado, bed.

- Label the faces of the dice 1, 2, 3, using each number twice.
- Lay hoops opposite one another, leaving a large gap between; if there are more than two players, lay the hoops in a circular pattern, equidistance apart.
- Divide the cards equally among the hoops and place face down inside the hoop area.
- Place a dice inside each hoop.

Rules

- On the call of *Six sizzling sausages,* players run clockwise round behind the hoops and back to their place.

- The first one back is the winner.

- The winner throws his dice to find a number and turns over one of the cards in the hoop.

- To win a point, he must think of the number of adjectives indicated on the dice to describe the noun on the card, e.g. *terrible, tricky, troublesome tigers.*

- The words must start with the same sound. E.g., *one* and *wheel* would be correct even though the words begin with different letters.

- If the player is unable to think of enough words to make alliteration, the player who came second has a turn.

Activity

- Explain to the children the rules of the game and have a practice go to ensure everyone understands.

- Play the game and award a point to the players who can correctly give the number of adjectives.

Extension

- Write alliteration about getting dressed to go outside on a cold day or a shopping list. In each case, start by making a list of the nouns, e.g. *wellies, gloves* or *watermelon tomatoes.*

I put on my	I bought
wacky, waterproof wellies	one wide watermelon
gorgeous glittering gloves	two tasty tomatoes
etc.	etc.

How do you feel?

This is a way to help children describe how a character is reacting to a particular situation.

This is a game for three or more players.

Resources

- Copy of page 84.
- One large label sticker for each child.
- Felt-tip pen.
- Pen or pencil for each child.

Preparation

- Photocopy page 84, one for each child and one extra.
- Choose an emotion for each child from the list below and write it on a sticker.
  - sad
  - frightened
  - cross
  - surprised
  - embarrassed
- Choose a different emotion for each player.

Before beginning the activity

- Choose an emotion for yourself, write it on a label or card and place it face down on the table.

- Say, *We are going to play a game called 'How Do you feel?' I have written a word that describes how I am feeling on this card. You have to work out what that feeling is by asking me questions. I can only answer 'yes' or 'no'.*

- Put a copy of the list of statements in the middle of the table for the group to see.

- Say, *Here are some words and phrases that authors use to show how characters are feeling. I want you to ask me questions so that you can work out what I am feeling. You will need to cross out some of the phrases or words as we go along.*

- Encourage the children to ask questions and show them how to work out which phrases/words to cross out, e.g. You have chosen *surprised* as the demonstration word.

  - Question: *Are you angry?*

  - Answer: *No.*

- Help the children identify which words/phrases could be crossed out (e.g. clenched his fists; snarled).

Activity

- As soon as the children have understood how the game works, stick an emotion label on to the back of each child and give each one a list and a pen.

- Ask the children to stand up and move around, as they can only ask one question from one person.

- As the children move around, check that they are crossing off the correct words on their lists.

Extension

- Write a paragraph.

- Give the children a choice of two named characters.

- Tell them that their character has just opened the door of the classroom and seen something that has made him . . . (choose an emotion).

- Ask the children to write three or four sentences about their character opening the door, what they see, and describe how they react, speak and move across the room.

How Do You Feel?

trembled	trembled	trembled
turned pale	turned pale	turned pale
blinked back the tears	blinked back the tears	blinked back the tears
stamped her foot	stamped her foot	stamped her foot
snarled	snarled	snarled
her mouth dropped open	her mouth dropped open	her mouth dropped open
he opened his eyes wide	he opened his eyes wide	he opened his eyes wide
blushed	blushed	blushed
lip trembled	lip trembled	lip trembled
hands shook	hands shook	hands shook
slammed the door	slammed the door	slammed the door
nearly jumped out of his skin	nearly jumped out of his skin	nearly jumped out of his skin
felt his face burn	felt his face burn	felt his face burn
scowled	scowled	scowled
turned the colour of a ripe tomato	turned the colour of a ripe tomato	turned the colour of a ripe tomato
tears in his eyes	tears in his eyes	tears in his eyes
dropped the plate and screamed	dropped the plate and screamed	dropped the plate and screamed
jumped up and down with delight	jumped up and down with delight	jumped up and down with delight
stomach tightened	stomach tightened	stomach tightened
the tips of her ears turned pink	the tips of her ears turned pink	the tips of her ears turned pink
clenched his fists	clenched his fists	clenched his fists

Guess the mood

This is a way to help children describe a character.

Resources

- Copies of emotion cards on pages 88 and 89.

- A copy of the game board on page 90.

- Whiteboard and pen.

Preparation

- Photocopy the game board on page 90, for each player.

- Photocopy pages 88 and 89 and cut up into cards.

- Write the following clauses on the whiteboard:

  - clapped his hands

  - sucked his thumb

  - his legs turned to jelly

  - bit his lip.

Before beginning the activity

- Show the whiteboard to the child and tell him these are words to describe how a character is feeling, two are ways of describing what we do with our bodies, and two show what we do with our faces.

- Ask him to choose the clause that shows the character is happy/worried/frightened.

Activity

- Give each player a copy of the game board and a triangular emotion card.

- Place circles face down in one pile and rectangles face down in a separate pile.

- Read the emotion card with the child – this card is the emotion the character is feeling.

- Tell the child the game is to find all the circle and rectangle cards which describe that emotion. The circle cards describe facial expressions and the rectangle cards describe body movements.

- Ask the child to begin by taking the top card from both piles.

- Read the words and, if they describe the emotion card, he can keep it; if not, make a discard pile.

- The first player to find all the cards for the character is the winner.

- Read the cards with the child.

- On the whiteboard, using as many words from the cards as possible, write a paragraph together.

- Give the character a name and choose one of the following situations:

  a. [Name] sat up in bed. What had woken him?

  b. [Name] heard the boy tell the others [name] had tripped him up on purpose.

  c. [Name] opened the letter.

  d. [Name] sat on the bench by himself/herself.

Extension

- Play the game with the child.

- When the game is finished, ask the child to write a description of the person as if he was watching him across a room.

Guess the Mood

Emotion cards

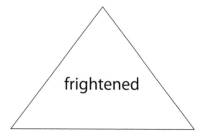

frightened

delighted

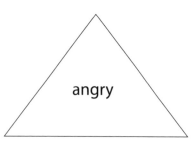

angry

miserable

mouth turned down at the corners	tears pricked his eyes	bottom lip trembled	stared at the floor
dragged one foot after the other	head drooped	shoulders hunched	huddles in a corner

© R Hickey 2010 *Thirty-three Ways to Help with Writing* Routledge

Guess the Mood

gritted teeth

foaming at the mouth

grew red

face as black as thunder

hot under the collar

clench fists

stamp foot

arms held stiffly

eyes darted about

turned pale

the colour drained from his face

bit back a scream

frozen to the spot

knees trembled

jumped out of his skin

legs turned to jelly

face split into a grin

grinned from ear to ear

laughed out loud

eyes sparkled

© R Hickey 2010 *Thirty-three Ways to Help with Writing* Routledge

Guess the Mood Game Board

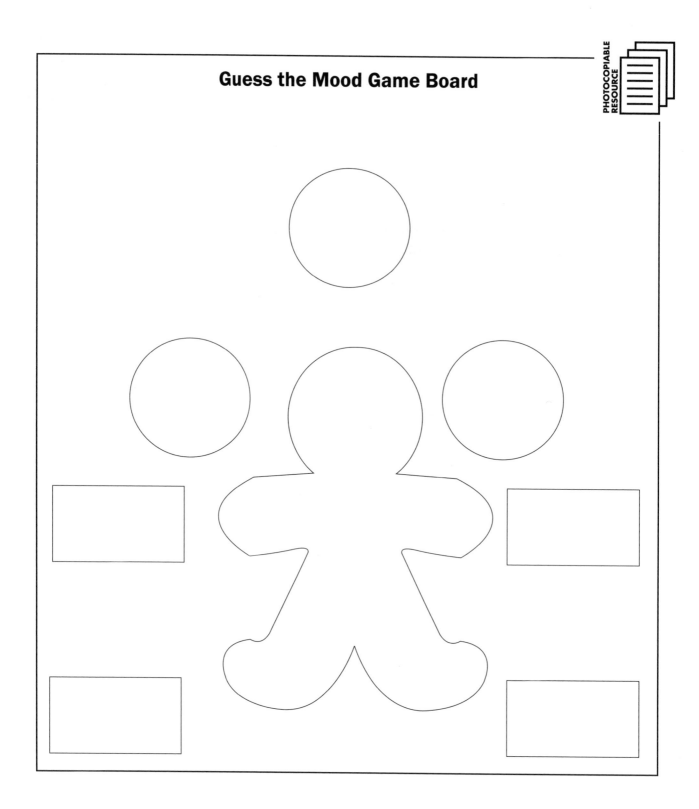

Castle adventure

This is a way to help children with characterisation by using speech.

A game for two to four players.

Resources

- A copy of the Castle adventure game board on page 93.

- A counter for each player.

- Dice.

Preparation

- Photocopy page 93 and either paste on to card or laminate.

Rules

- Play begins at the top of the board. The players throw the dice and move the appropriate number of squares.

- When a player lands on a square containing a problem, he must speak about it in character as described below.

Activity

- Describe the following scenario to the child: *Two [three or four] children have discovered a crumbling old castle deep in the woods. The front door is locked but they manage to climb a tree and get on to the roof where they find an unlocked door. All of the children feel differently about the adventure.*

  - *One doesn't like doing anything wrong and thinks they shouldn't have come into the woods in the first place.*

  - *One encouraged the others to explore the woods, but is now beginning to get scared.*

  - *One is getting braver as the adventure goes on.*

  - *One is scared of everything.*

- Ask the child to be one of the characters (or you decide: suggest roles as appropriate).

  - Ask, *What would that character say when they found the locked door? What would (another character) say as they climbed the tree?*

- Tell the child that the game is about what happens inside the castle. Ask the child to choose which character he is going to be.

- Explain that when his counter lands on a square that has a problem written in it, his character has to discuss the problem with the other player(s).

Extension

- Choose one line from the game board.

- Ask the child to write a paragraph describing the children's progress through that part of the castle. Include what one of the characters said and what one replied.

Castle Adventure Game Board

					Doorway in
Fell through the floor			Heard a clanking sound	Passage is very dark	← ↓
	→	Found a candle		Hear squeaking noises in the wall	Leant on the wall and opened a secret passage
Stand on a squeaky floor board		Hear faint voices		Enter a bedroom. Someone is snoring	←
	→	A mouse runs over your foot	A wind blows from nowhere		Candle blows out
The passage forks to the left and right		Trip over a rusty chain		Ran into spiders web	←
	→ Hear footsteps		A guard sees you		Doorway out

© R Hickey 2010 *Thirty-three Ways to Help with Writing* Routledge

Talk, talk, talk

This is a way to help children use speech to add information about a character.

Resources

- Photocopy of sentences on page 96.

- Four squares of paper or whiteboards.

- A pen.

Preparation

- Write the following phrases on the four pieces of paper, one phrase on each:

    - An impatient person

    - A tired person

    - A worried person

    - A person who bullies others.

Activity

- Show the child the cards. Read the words and discuss what an impatient, tired or worried person, or a person who bullies might say.

- Display the four cards in four separate areas in the room.

- Say, *I am going to read you a sentence one of these characters has said. When I have read it, I want you to decide whether the person is impatient, worried, tired or is a person who bullies others, then go and stand by the right label.*

- Read out the first of the following speeches.

- Ask the child to move to the corner displaying the word to describe the character.

Extension

- Ask the child to think of different moods which the characters could have. Choose a mood, and ask the child to write down what the character would say in one of the situations described below.

- Choose one of the following situations:

  - Someone is late.

  - The character has been walking for a long time.

  - The character is sitting at a table where the people sitting with him are arguing.

  - A sudden noise wakes him in the night.

Repeat with a different mood and/or a different situation.

Talk Talk Talk Sentences

"Come on, we haven't got all day." **impatient**	"You are such a cry-baby." **bullying**	"Fancy being scared of a frog." **bullying**
"I'm going right now. I'm not waiting any longer." **impatient**	"Put the kettle on, would you?" **tired**	"Here, give me a hand with this." **tired**
"Oh dear, we're going to be late." **worried**	"Where can it have got to?" **worried**	"Let me do it, you're too slow." **impatient**
"That haircut makes you look like a girl." **bullying**	"Just give me five minutes to put my feet up." **tired**	"But won't she be very angry with you?" **worried**

D. Exploring different forms of writing

Non-fiction

These activities are best suited for those children who have attained National Curriculum level 3 and are working towards level 4.

In non-fiction the writing structure and format vary according to the purpose of the text; however, improving children's non-fiction writing demands the same underlying principles as for fiction: choosing precise nouns and verbs and being able to begin sentences and paragraphs in different ways, using linking connectives and adverbs. Therefore many of the activities in the previous sections are useful for non-fiction writing.

There are five major non-fiction formats included in the teaching of literacy, each one having its own format (explanation, recount, report, persuasion, instruction). For this reason the activities included in the non-fiction section focus on language common to a number of writing formats, or the differences between them.

Lingo

This is a way to help children use appropriate language in non-fiction writing.

Resources

- A copy of the Lingo game board on page 102.

- Six counters for each child.

Preparation

- Photocopy page 102 and cut up into sections (one for each child). Either paste on to card or laminate.

Rules

- The teacher reads the texts (in any order) given below. The child identifies the type of non-fiction writing and places a counter over the name if it is on his card.

- The game ends when the player has a counter in each square.

Activity

- Read from the following writing formats. **Do not read the extracts in order** as they are grouped in writing types. You will need to choose and read sentences from each writing format in order for the children to play the game.

Instructions

1. You will need a balloon, a cardboard box, scissors and sellotape.

2. Stir the mixture briskly.

3. Your rabbit needs a warm, safe place to sleep in.

4. Put a bowl of fresh water into the cage every day.

5. Eat five portions of fruit or vegetables every day.

Explanations

1. As the hot air rises, it meets cold air. This causes clouds to form.

2. When the wheel turns, the buckets attached to the wheel enter the water. The turning of the wheel allows the buckets to scoop up water.

3. Warmer weather brings less winter snow, so animals that would normally be unable live at this height are able to make their homes higher up the mountain.

4. Rivers are also important for farming because river valleys and plains provide fertile soil. Farmers in dry regions irrigate their cropland using water carried by irrigation ditches from nearby rivers.

5. A river bends as it adjusts to things like a change in the current, or obstacles.

Reports

1. Baby Trolls are born with small pointed bumps on their foreheads which grow into horns. As a troll grows older, the horns twist and curl.

2. The dullahan is one of the most spectacular creatures in Irish stories. Around midnight on certain Irish festival or feast days, this wild and black-robed horseman may be seen riding a dark, snorting horse across the countryside.

3. The mass of spikes has been designed to stand up to gusts of wind travelling at more than 100 miles per hour. The steel used in its construction will change colour over time because of the weather.

4. Masatonga, 19, became a hero yesterday when he succeeded in killing the fierce dragon which has been terrorising the county for the past month.

5. Yesterday a foot was discovered in a block of peat being transported to a shredding mill in Cheshire. The foot was found when Andy Mould, a workman at the factory, threw a piece of peat at a work mate.

Recounts

1. I thought Spain was the most exciting country I had visited, with the most dramatic collection of art in the world. This particular visit made me look at light and shade in paintings in a new way.

2. While we were there, we saw paintings by Picasso and other artists of the time. We had a go at copying their style.

3. We were lucky enough to be able to watch them painting the finished pots. After that we painted our own pots.

4. When we entered the museum it was very quiet and dark. Our guide took us to the top floor where the Egyptian mummies are kept.

5. Today has been a horrible day. I got into trouble at school even though it wasn't my fault. Perry put a drawing pin through my ribbon and when I went to stand up, my hair was pinned to the chair.

Persuasion

1. If you thought Switzerland was only for winter skiing holidays, think again.

   At Englebraum we have the perfect facilities for walking, climbing and mountain bike riding.

2. The fact is that the rooms are small, dark and cold. The walls are damp and when it rains, water leaks through the roof. Surely no one would expect people to live in these flats.

3. This should become a problem for the police. We should not have to put up with such dangerous behaviour. It has become too big a problem to be ignored.

4. About a thousand people are crammed into this refugee camp where there is little food or water. If we do not act immediately, people will die of hunger and disease.

5. I've always thought her books were quite boring. But I was very surprised by *Count to Ten*. The characters were interesting and so was the story line. It is a truly unique book.

Extension

● Ask the child to choose one of the types of writing. Ask him to choose one of the examples and to add another sentence or two in the same style.

Lingo Game Board

recount	report	explanation
instructions	persuasion	recount

recount	report	explanation
report	explanation	recount

explanation	report	explanation
instructions	persuasion	recount

recount	report	persuasion
instructions	persuasion	recount

Musical halves

This is a way to help children recognise the different styles of non-fiction writing.

This is a game for four to six children.

Resources

- A chair for each child.

- A copy of Musical halves recounts on page 105 and Reports on page 106.

- A musical instrument such as a triangle or a drum.

Preparation

- Photocopy pages 105 and 106 and cut up into cards.

- Put the Report cards face down on each chair.

Activity

- Explain to the children that they are going to play a game like musical chairs, the difference being that there are enough chairs for everyone.

- Ask them to walk around to the beat of the musical instrument. When it stops, ask them to pick up the card from the nearest chair and sit down.

- Ask them to read the text and then to find someone else who has the second part of the text.

- Ask the group if they are able to tell you what type of writing it is.

- Repeat the game with cards from Recounts.

Extension

- Choose a recount, report or explanation text and copy two or three sentences on to a card.

- Repeat to make enough cards to give one to each child.

- Ask the children to read their cards and write the second half on another card to make up their own game of Musical halves.

Musical Halves

Recount

I couldn't wait for school to be over today. Mrs Harry asked me why I was so fidgety.	We are having a great time here. You know I wasn't very keen to come; I really wanted to go on holiday with my friend Grace.
It was because I was going to my cousin's birthday as soon as school finished.	However it is lovely here. We have been learning how to sail little boats. They are so small there is only room for one person.
Yesterday it was my turn to choose our family day out. I chose to go to the zoo. It is my favourite place. I love to watch the monkeys.	I've always loved drawing. My Nana bought me a huge book of blank pages and I filled it in a month.
We had to go to the zoo yesterday. Polly knows I would rather go fishing on the lake, but it was her turn to choose. Of course she made us all go to watch the monkeys.	I loved art at secondary school. We had a brilliant teacher who often let me carry on with my work after school.

Musical Halves Reports

Roofs and houses were damaged last night when winds gusting up to 70mph battered the town.	Have you seen the film *The Pirates of the Caribbean?* Did you know there used to be a lot of pirates around the Caribbean in the 16th and 17th centuries?
One of the worst affected areas was in the northern part of Woolstock. Mr Jones said he had never experienced anything like it.	There were plenty of deserted islands where the pirates could live; and there were a lot of treasure ships sailing past on their way to Spain.
Two men were rescued last night after they were swept out to sea while fishing from the pier.	Robots have been around for many years, but most of them do not look at all like the ones in Science Fiction films.
Rescuers were afraid that one of the men, Andrew Carter, had drowned but he was found clinging to a rock.	Factories which have assembly lines use robots the most. Each robot is designed to do a different job.

Muddled emails

This is a way to help children recognise the language used in non-fiction writing.

Resources

- A non-fiction reading book.

- A fiction reading book.

- Highlighter pen.

Preparation

- Copy one or two sentences from the non-fiction book, followed by sentences from the fiction story, followed by non-fiction, etc., until the text resembles the following:

    The River Thames flows through the city. Billy looked around. He had no idea where he was.

    The London Eye was built by the river. People can go on it and see a bird's eye view of London. He could see the mangled tail of his space craft half buried in the hill. Before he knew what was happening, he was snatched up and dragged away. The Houses of Parliament are on the other side of the river. The bell inside the big clock is called Big Ben.

- Repeat, mixing the two texts, until you have about half to three-quarters of a page of text.

Activity

- Show the child the text and explain that somehow two emails became muddled together and sent as one text.

- Read the passage through with the child.

- Talk about the two types of writing the child can see.

- Help the child find the sentences which belong to the non-fiction text. Ask the child to highlight them as he reads. Allow him to continue independently when he understands the task.

Extension

- Use the same task but muddle two non-fiction texts.

- To make the task even harder, mix parts of a sentence with fiction and non-fiction.

    E.g.

    The River Thames Billy looked around flows through the city. He had the London Eye was built by the river no idea where he was.

    People can go on it and see a bird's eye view he could see the mangled tail of London of his space craft half buried in the hill.

Information, information, information

This is a way to help children notice the style and language used in non-fiction writing.

Resources

● Copies of Information, information, information on pages 112 and 113.

Preparation

● Photocopy Information, information, information on pages 112 and 113 and cut up into cards. Label the backs of cards A with A and the B cards with B.

● Spread the cards in rows face down on the table.

Activity

● Ask the child to turn over an A and a B card and read the two cards. If the two cards belong together (i.e. they are both part of the same writing type), he keeps the cards and has another turn.

● The winner is the player with the most pairs at the end of the game.

● The answers are on page 114.

Extension

- Explain to the child that you are going to read out some information. Ask the child to listen and decide whether he thinks the person who wrote it sounds authoritative (i.e. as if he knows what he is talking about). Ask the child to give a reason for his answer.

1. Kapok (kay – pock) comes from a tree. You can make clothes out of kapok. People get the kapok and then they turn it into material like cotton.

   Answer: *No. Information texts should not use 'you'. The verbs 'get' and 'turn' are weak, they are not descriptive enough. The last sentence uses a weak connective 'then' and the information is vague.*

2. Some butterflies can fly incredible distances. In North America at the start of autumn, swarms of Monarch butterflies migrate south to spend the winter in Mexico, a distance of almost 2000 kilometres. When spring returns to the north, they begin the long journey back again.

   Answer: *Yes. Use of technical language – swarms, migrate, distance. The style is impersonal. Precise information – name of butterfly, where it comes from, where it goes, length of flight.*

3. Salmon are the most amazing fish I have heard of. They swim up rivers to breed. I saw a programme on TV once and there was a bear catching salmon. The salmon jumped out of the water.

   Answer: *No. Style is personal because the author uses 'I'. There is only one sentence which gives information. Three sentences are not relevant.*

4. Scientists studying Ancient Egyptian scrolls, read about a city called Herakleion near the river Nile. But it isn't there anymore. Some divers dived to the bottom of the river and found it.

   Answer: *No. There is not enough information. The sentences are simple and joined with weak connectives.*

5. Rabbits are a nuisance to farmers. They dig holes and eat all the grass. Some people want to poison them. I think that is a good idea but my friend says it is cruel.

Answer: *No. Style is personal because the author uses 'I' and 'my'. The writer gives a little information but then gives a personal opinion. The sentences are all short.*

6. Frogs require damp, shady conditions. Some frogs are in danger of becoming extinct because of drought and fire.

   Answer: *Yes. Use of technical language – require, conditions, extinct. Style is impersonal. Adjectives give more information – damp and shady. Gives reason for extinction.*

7. Millions of birds make amazing journeys every year. One tiny bird, that weighs about the same as a box of matches, flies from Africa to Britain every spring and returns every autumn. It is called a willow warbler.

   Answer: *Yes. The style is impersonal. Precise information – name of bird, where it comes from, where it goes, weight.*

8. Poor children in Victorian Times played in the street. Poor children played with dolls. The dolls were made out of wood. Poor children had whistles too. The whistles were made out of tin. Rich children had nurseries. Rich children had horses.

   Answer: *No. The writer gives information but writes short sentences, starting each sentence in similar ways. The writing doesn't flow, so it sounds as if the writer doesn't know much about the topic.*

9. Vikings came to Britain to steal. They had the best ships. They were very brave.

   Answer: *No. The facts are not related to each other. The sentences are all short; therefore the writing doesn't flow, so it sounds as if the writer doesn't know much about the topic.*

The hotel is close to the sea and the lively town of San Moreno.	Check into the Torrent River Hotel and enjoy a holiday packed with adventure.
Have you ever watched a puddle dry up in the sun and wondered where the water goes?	Did you know these facts about water? The Pacific Ocean covers nearly a third of the Earth's surface.
Council members voted last night to bring in a by-law banning skateboarding from the town centre.	Obstacles come in all shapes and sizes. Banks are ramps with a gradual, even slope.
A flash flood happens when a wall of water quickly sweeps over an area.	Louise began training Benjy when he was three months old. First he had to learn 'heal', 'sit', and 'stay'.
Saxon houses were dark and smoky. The cooking fire was built in the middle of the room.	The Celts worshipped many gods. The priests were called Druids. They sacrificed animals to tell the future.
Yesterday a foot was discovered in a block of peat.	Scientists have discovered that Lindow Man had been hit on the crown of his head.

Information, Information, Information Cards B

This pleasant, comfortable hotel has two swimming pools, mini-golf and a shop.	Take a 9km trek on horseback or waterski on the huge lake 100 metres from the hotel.
In the hot sun, water evaporates. It rises into the air to form clouds.	The longest river is the River Nile. It flows from Uganda, through Sudan to Egypt and into the Mediterranean sea.
"Skateboarders have extensively damaged the stonework on steps and benches," town centre manager Allan Buckley reported.	Quarter-pipe and half-pipe ramps have very steep, curved slopes. They are great for gaining speed quickly.
People can also cause floods too by replacing grass and dirt with concrete or paving.	Next Louise played hide-and-seek with Benjy. He was very quick to learn.
The smoke drifted up to the roof and out through the thatch.	They believed everything alive was made up of four things: air, fire, earth, water.
A police spokesman said "It is impossible to tell how old this body is".	He also had a beard and his fingernails had been cut with scissors.

Answers to Information, Information, Information

Cards A	Cards B
The hotel is close to the sea and the lively town of San Moreno.	This pleasant, comfortable hotel has two swimming pools, mini-golf and a shop.
Have you ever watched a puddle dry up in the sun and wondered where the water goes?	In the hot sun, water evaporates. It rises into the air to form clouds.
Council members voted last night to bring in a by-law banning skateboarding from the town centre.	"Skateboarders have extensively damaged the stonework on steps and benches," town centre manager Allan Buckley reported.
A flash flood happens when a wall of water quickly sweeps over an area.	People can also cause floods by replacing grass and dirt with concrete or paving.
Saxon houses were dark and smoky. The cooking fire was built in the middle of the room.	The smoke drifted up to the roof and out through the thatch.
Yesterday a foot was discovered in a block of peat.	A police spokesman said "It is impossible to tell how old this body is".
Check into the Torrent River Hotel and enjoy a holiday packed with adventure.	Take a 9km trek on horseback or waterski on the huge lake 100 metres from the hotel.
Did you know these facts about water? The Pacific Ocean covers nearly a third of the Earth's surface.	The longest river is the River Nile. It flows from Uganda, through Sudan to Egypt and into the Mediterranean sea.
Obstacles for skateboarders come in all shapes and sizes. Banks are ramps with a gradual, even slope.	Quarter-pipe and half-pipe ramps have very steep, curved slopes: great for gaining speed quickly.
Louise began training Benjy when he was three months old. First he had to learn 'heal', 'sit', and 'stay'.	Next Louise played hide-and-seek with Benjy. He was very quick to learn.
The Celts worshipped many gods. The priests were called Druids and sacrificed animals.	They believed everything alive was made up of four things: air, fire, earth, water.
Scientists have discovered that Lindow Man had been hit on the crown of his head.	He also had a beard and his fingernails had been cut with scissors.

20 questions

This is a way to help children distinguish between different types of non-fiction writing.

A game for two or more players.

Resources

- A copy of 20 questions board on page 118.

- A counter for each player.

Preparation

- Photocopy the 20 questions game board on page 118 and either paste on to card or laminate.

Rules

- Players must answer a question correctly before they can make a move.

- When an answer is correct, move forward three spaces.

- For an incorrect response, move back one space.

Activity

- In this game the teacher asks the questions and cannot participate.

- **Do not read the questions in order** as they are grouped in writing types. You will need to choose the most appropriate questions for the children.

- Tell the children they are going to play a game where they can only move their counter if they can answer a question correctly. All the questions are about writing non-fiction.

Questions

- If you were writing a recount, would you write? *we are going* or *we went*

  Answer: we went

- Which of these is a time connective? *until, because, after*

  Answer: after

- Can you use *I* or *you* in instructions?

  Answer: no

- Is a diary a type of recount?

  Answer: yes

- Name a type of writing where things must be written in chronological order (you do one thing and then the next).

  Answer: instructions recounts (usually), explanations

- Name the writing you would choose to write a recipe.

  Answer: instructions

- Which of these verbs is the odd one out? *put, mix, went, take*

  Answer: went

- What type of writing would have a heading? *materials needed*

  Answer: instructions

- What type of writing would have a heading? *habitat*

  Answer: report

- Which title does not belong? *How to play statues, Mountains, Making your own book*

  Answer: mountains

- Name a type of writing where you could use a diagram.

  Answer: instructions, report, explanation

- Name a type of writing where you must use the present tense, e.g. *live, eat, not lived* or *ate*

  Answer: report, explanation

- Name the type of writing in which you are most likely to use technical words like, *prey, camouflage*

  Answer: report or explanation

- If you were writing a report, would you write *jump* or *jumped*?

  Answer: jump

- Where would you find this type of writing? *A boy of 6 has been suspended from school because of his haircut.*

  Answer: a newspaper

- If you were writing a poster to tell people about your school fair, what information must you include?

  Answer: any one of the following: time, date, place

- What word could you add to this sentence to make it more persuasive. *Come and see the elephant . . .*

  Answer: accept any appropriate adjective

- What type of writing would have the title *Children should do more homework*?

  Answer: persuasive

- Which title would not belong to an explanation text?
  Healthy eating, How to grow beans, Why volcanoes erupt.

  Answer: healthy eating

- When writing an explanation would you use the present tense or the past tense, e.g. *occurs, happens* or *occurred, happened*?

  Answer: present tense

Extension

- Read some of the questions from the game again.

- Ask the child to think of other similar questions to play the game with a friend.

20 Questions Game Board

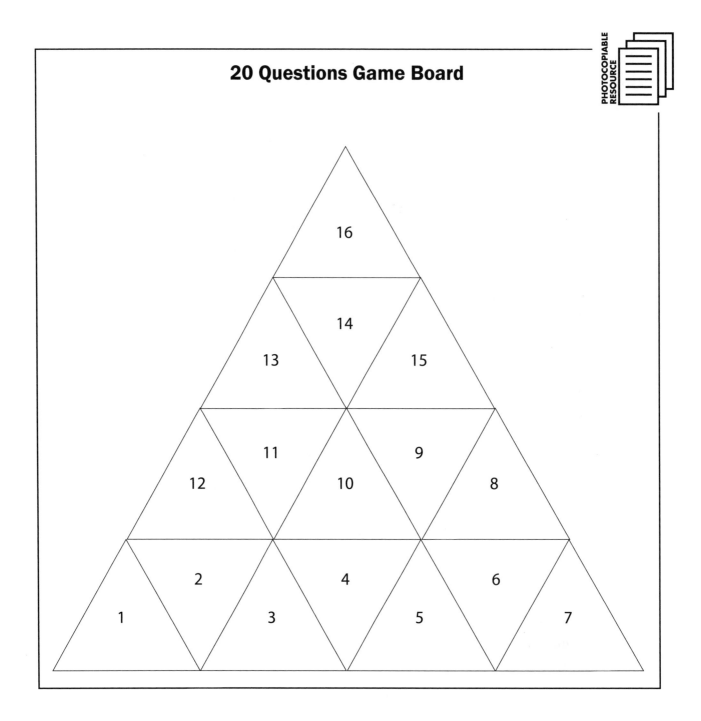

A technical crossword

This is one way to help children learn the language used in non-fiction writing.

Resources

- A copy of the blank crossword on page 121.

- A pencil.

- A thesaurus.

Preparation

- Photocopy page 121.

Activity

- Talk about what a crossword is, and how to write one letter in each square.

- Show him the two clues; the first is a synonym for the clue, the second is a sentence. The number in brackets indicates the number of letters.

- Help the child fill in the crossword, showing him how the letters from one clue help with another one.

- Use the thesaurus to search for a synonym of the clue word if the child cannot think of the answer.

The answers are given below.

Extension

- Show the child how to make a simple three-word crossword.

- Choose three words from a non-fiction text. You will need words that have varying numbers of letters with one letter in common between pairs of words.

- Write one word across the middle of the squared paper.

- Choose another word to go down from it, putting the letter common to both at the start, middle or end of the second word.

- Add another word across the bottom, using the last letter of the down word as a letter common to both words.

- Number the squares where the words begin.

- Write clues for the words across and words down in separate lists.

- At the end of each clue, write the number of letters in the word.

- When the child has completed his crossword, he can give it to a friend to fill in.

Crossword Answers

Across	Down
1 camouflage	2 discover
3 form	3 flee
5 prey	4 extinct

A Technical Crossword

Across

1	disguise	Animals can hide from their enemies by using _____ (10)
3	make	When water droplets get very cold they _____ ice (4)
5	eat	Lions _____ on deer (4)

Down

2	find	Scientists _____ new information (7)
3	run away	When animals are being hunted they _____ (4)
4	all dead	The dinosaurs are _____ (7)

Glossary

Adjective an adjective is a word that describes a person or an object. Adjectives come before the person or object they are describing, as in:

Conrad helped the old man   The gold leaves lay on the ground

or after linking verbs such as be, look, get, seem, as in:

This shoe seems bigger   The dinner looks delicious
I am hungry   James gets cross when he is tired

Adverb an adverb gives additional meaning to a verb, an adjective or another adverb:

The man walked slowly verb + adverb
The boy's coat was extremely dirty adverb + adjective
The man walked really slowly adverb + adverb

An adverb can move around in a sentence:

Quietly, the man walked into the house.
The man *quietly* walked into the house.
The man walked into the house *quietly*.

Adverbial phrase a group of words that works in the same way as one adverb:

We went to the cinema *a few days ago*.

An adverbial phrase can move around in a sentence.

Alliteration a phrase where words together begin with the same sound.

Antonym a word with a meaning opposite to another:

Big – small tall - short

Clause a group of words that contain a verb. A simple sentence is a clause:

I went out.

Some clauses cannot stand alone:

I went out when it was raining.

Connective a word that links sentences or clauses together.

Metaphor a writer uses his imagination to write about a subject as if it were something else:

Razor back cliffs *steepled* into the sky.

Noun a word that denotes someone or something.

Phrase a group of words that go together but do not contain a verb:

in the morning: as young as you.

Simile a sentence where the writer compares a subject to something else:

The mist rose off the mountains like a cover being removed from a painting.

Synonym a word that has the same or a very similar meaning to another:

big/huge.

Verb a word for an action, or a happening. It is often described as a 'doing' or 'being' word.

Verb chain two or more words that make a verb phrase:

are going, have been going.